Jermaine Dye

and the CHICAGO WHITE SOX

2005 WORLD SERIES

by Michael Sandler

Consultant: Jim Sherman
Head Baseball Coach
University of Delaware

BEARPORT
PUBLISHING

New York, New York

Credits

Cover and Title Page, © Johnathan Daniel/Getty Images; 4, © Rob Tringali/SportsChrome/ newscom; 5, © Rich Pilling/MLB Photos via Getty Images; 6, © National Baseball Hall of Fame Library/MLB Photos via Getty Images; 7T, © Bettmann/CORBIS; 7B, © New York Times Co./Getty Images; 8, © AP Images/Charles Rex Arbogast; 9, © AP Images/Mark Lennihan; 10, © AP Images/Ed Zurga; 11, © REUTERS/Mike Blake; 12, © Jonathan Daniel/Getty Images; 13, © AP Images/Jeff Roberson; 14, © Jed Jacobsohn/Getty Images; 15, © Jed Jacobsohn/ Getty Images; 16, © Jed Jacobsohn/Getty Images; 17, © Brad Mangin/MLB Photos via Getty Images; 18, © Brad Mangin/MLB Photos via Getty Images; 19, © REUTERS/Lucy Nicholson; 20, © AP Photo/Amy Sancetta; 21, © Stephen Dunn/Getty Images; 22T, © Brian Bahr/Getty Images; 22C, © Otto Greule Jr/Getty Images; 22B, © Lisa Blumenfeld/Getty Images.

Publisher: Kenn Goin
Senior Editor: Lisa Wiseman
Creative Director: Spencer Brinker
Design: Stacey May
Photo Researcher: James O'Connor

Library of Congress Cataloging-in-Publication Data

Sandler, Michael.
 Jermaine Dye and the Chicago White Sox : 2005 World Series / by Michael Sandler.
    p. cm. — (World Series superstars)
 Includes bibliographical references and index.
 ISBN-13: 978-1-59716-637-9 (library binding)
 ISBN-10: 1-59716-637-5 (library binding)
 1. Dye, Jermaine, 1974—Juvenile literature. 2. Baseball players—United States—Biography—Juvenile literature. 3. Chicago White Sox (Baseball team)—Juvenile literature. I. Title.

 GV865.D94S36 2008
 796.357092—dc22
 (B)
                                   2007031492

For more information, write to Bearport Publishing Company, Inc., 101 Fifth Avenue, Suite 6R, New York, New York 10003. Printed in the United States of America.

10 9 8 7 6 5 4 3 2 1

★ Contents ★

The Long Wait

Chicago fans had been waiting 88 years for the White Sox to win the World Series. Now, in Game 4 of the 2005 World Series, the team's long losing **streak** was about to end. Chicago needed only one run to beat the Houston Astros and win the **title**.

Could Chicago get the needed run? It was up to right fielder Jermaine Dye. In the batter's box, he waited for the pitch. Then he swung.

Fans rooting for the Chicago White Sox

Jermaine at bat
in Game 4

The Chicago White Sox hadn't
won a World Series since 1917.

The Curse

Why hadn't Chicago won in so many years? Many people blamed a **curse** that began in 1919. That year Chicago lost the World Series to the Cincinnati Reds.

Soon, a shocking secret came out. Several White Sox players had actually been trying to lose. **Gamblers** paid them to drop balls, make bad throws, and strike out. After that World Series, the White Sox never won another title.

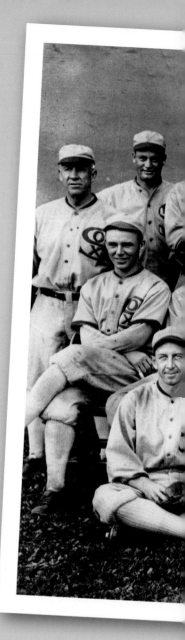

"Shoeless" Joe Jackson was the star of the 1919 White Sox.

The 1919 Chicago White Sox

The players who were paid to lose were not allowed to play in the **major leagues** for the rest of their lives.

Jermaine Arrives

When Jermaine Dye joined the White Sox in 2005, he knew all about the curse. He just didn't believe in it. If he had, he wouldn't have come to Chicago from the Oakland A's.

The big-hitting outfielder was a **free agent**. Many teams wanted him. They offered him a lot of money. Jermaine turned them all down to play for the White Sox.

Jermaine liked the team. He thought Chicago had a good chance of winning the World Series.

Jermaine at his first spring training with the White Sox

The first major-league team Jermaine played for was the Atlanta Braves in 1996. He homered during his very first time at bat.

Jermaine at bat for the Atlanta Braves

Ozzie Believes

White Sox manager Ozzie Guillen thought they could win, too. He had high hopes for the 2005 season.

Chicago didn't have many **All-Stars**, but Ozzie believed in his players. He counted on his pitchers to throw the ball well. He counted on his fielders to play good **defense**.

If everyone does their share, thought Ozzie, we will win a lot of games. Most of the time, a run or two is all that's needed.

Ozzie hoped for strong pitching from players such as José Contreras.

Ozzie (right) talking with Jermaine (left) in the dugout

Before becoming manager, Ozzie had played **shortstop** for the White Sox.

First Place

Ozzie was right. Sometimes one run was just enough to win. In 2005, the White Sox proved this on **opening day**. The team moved into first place with a 1-0 victory over the Cleveland Indians. By mid-season, the White Sox led their **division** by 15 games.

Jermaine was playing well, too. After a slow start, he was slamming home runs and knocking in runners. Often, he gave Chicago the big hit they needed to win.

Fans eager to watch the White Sox play on opening day

In 2005, Jermaine's 31 home runs were the most for any right fielder.

Jermaine safely slides across home plate.

The Playoffs

The White Sox held on to first place all season long. In the **playoffs**, they **swept** their first **opponents**, the Boston Red Sox.

Next up were the Anaheim Angels. Chicago lost the opener, 3-2, but won the next four games. Nobody could believe it. They were going to the World Series!

All over Chicago, fans began to think the impossible. Could this be the year? Would the White Sox finally end their losing streak?

Freddy Garcia winds up to deliver a pitch during Game 4 of the playoffs against the Anaheim Angels.

Chicago celebrates their victory over the Angels.

Against Anaheim, White Sox **starters** threw four straight **complete games**.

The Rocket

Chicago's opponents in the 2005 World Series were the Houston Astros. The Astros were led by star pitcher Roger "the Rocket" Clemens. No pitch in baseball was tougher to hit than the Rocket's speeding **fastball**.

In the first inning of Game 1, the Rocket threw a fastball straight down the middle to Jermaine. Jermaine smacked it for a homer. Chicago went on to beat the Astros, 5-3.

Roger Clemens had played in five World Series and won seven Cy Young Awards.

Jermaine watches as the ball he hit against Roger Clemens sails out of the stadium.

Jermaine wasn't just a great hitter, he was also an amazing outfielder. He even won a **Gold Glove** Award in 2000.

Almost There

As the series went on, each White Sox player did his share to help the team. Outfielder Scott Podsednik hadn't homered in the regular season. In Game 2, however, he smashed a **walk-off homer** to give Chicago the win.

Game 3 went 14 innings. Ozzie ran short of players and put **reserve** infielder Geoff Blum into the game. Geoff came through with a game-winning home run!

Now Chicago had three victories. One more and they would win the World Series once again.

Scott Podsednik runs the bases after hitting a home run.

Geoff Blum (right) gets a high five from his teammate, Freddy Garcia, after hitting the game-winning home run.

Game 3 lasted for 5 hours and 41 minutes. It was the longest in World Series history.

Champions

Game 4 was scoreless for the first seven innings. Then, with two men out in the eighth, Jermaine stepped to the plate.

Jermaine swung his bat and cracked a **grounder** up the middle. Teammate Willie Harris ran home from third base. Safe! The Sox led, 1-0!

The single run was all Jermaine and the White Sox needed. An inning later, a great roar echoed through Chicago's streets. The White Sox had won. The city could finally celebrate after 88 long years.

Jermaine hits a grounder
in the eighth inning of Game 4.

The White Sox
celebrate their victory!

DYE
23

Chicago Chi

PEREZ
7

After the game, Jermaine was
named Most Valuable Player
(MVP) of the 2005 World Series.

Jermaine, along with some other key players, helped the Chicago White Sox win the 2005 World Series.

Jermaine Dye #23

Right Field

Bats: Right Throws: Right
Born: 1/28/1974 in Vacaville, California
Height: 6'5" (1.96 m)
Weight: 240 pounds (109 kg)

Series Highlight
Drove in the winning run in Game 4

Paul Konerko #14

First Base

Bats: Right Throws: Right
Born: 3/5/1976 in Providence, Rhode Island
Height: 6'2" (1.88 m)
Weight: 215 pounds (97 kg)

Series Highlight
Hit a grand slam home run in Game 2

José Contreras #52

Starting Pitcher

Bats: Right Throws: Right
Born: 12/6/1971 in Las Martinas, Cuba
Height: 6'4" (1.93 m)
Weight: 245 pounds (111 kg)

Series Highlight
Pitched the White Sox to victory in Game 1

☆ Glossary ☆

All-Stars (AWL-STARZ) players chosen by the fans to play in baseball's yearly All-Star Game

complete games (kuhm-PLEET GAYMZ) games in which the starting pitcher pitches for the entire nine innings

curse (KURSS) something that brings or causes evil or misfortune

defense (DEE-fenss) players whose job it is to keep the other team from scoring

division (di-VIZH-uhn) a group of teams that compete against one another for a playoff spot

fastball (FAST-bawl) a pitch thrown as hard and quickly as possible

free agent (FREE AY-juhnt) a player who is not signed to any team and can choose which team to join

gamblers (GAM-blerz) people who bet money on a team

Gold Glove (GOHLD GLUHV) an award given to players for their outstanding fielding skills

grounder (GROUND-ur) a ball that is hit and rolls on the ground toward the outfield

major leagues (MAY-jur LEEGZ) the highest level of professional baseball teams in the United States, made up of the National League and the American League

opening day (OH-puh-ning DAY) the first game of a new baseball season

opponents (uh-POH-nuhnts) teams or athletes who others play against in a sporting event

playoffs (PLAY-awfss) the final games that determine which teams will play in the World Series

reserve (ree-ZURV) a player who doesn't usually play

shortstop (SHORT-stop) the player whose position is between second and third base

starters (START-urz) pitchers who play at the beginning of games

streak (STREEK) a long stretch of winning or losing

swept (SWEPT) won all the games in a series

title (TYE-tuhl) the championship; in baseball, a World Series win

walk-off homer (WAWK-awf HOME-ur) a home run that ends a game and brings victory to the team of the player who hit it

Bibliography

Verducci, Tom. "Isn't It Grand!" *Sports Illustrated* (November 4, 2005).

Chicago Sun-Times

The New York Times

Read More

O'Hearn, Michael. *The Story of the Chicago White Sox.* Mankato, MN: Creative Education (2007).

Stewart, Mark. *The Chicago White Sox.* Chicago: Norwood House (2006).

Learn More Online

To learn more about Jermaine Dye,
the Chicago White Sox, and the World Series, visit
www.bearportpublishing.com/WorldSeriesSuperstars

Index